Task-Based Listening

Task-Based Listening

What Every ESL Teacher Needs to Know

Steven Brown

University of Michigan Press
Ann Arbor

First paperback edition 2023
Copyright © Steven Brown, 2019
All rights reserved
Published in the United States of America by the
University of Michigan Press
Printed and bound by CPI Group (UK) Ltd, Croydon, CR0 4YY

Paperback ISBN: 978-0-472-03947-0
Ebook ISBN: 978-0-472-12564-7

First published December 2018

ACKNOWLEDGMENTS

Thanks to Kelly Sippell and her team at the University of Michigan Press. It is always a pleasure to work with them.

Thanks to Mike Rost and Marc Helgesen, for over thirty years of conversations about listening.

ACKNOWLEDGMENTS

CONTENTS

Introduction: The Purpose and Scope of This Book

Task-Based Listening: What Every ESL Needs to Know is a volume in the University of Michigan Press's *What Every ESL Teacher Needs to Know* series. As such, it gives the working teacher or teacher-in-training information about the basics of one important ESL field, in this case, listening.

Listening is one of the classic "big four" skills, along with reading, writing, and speaking. Listening skills are sometimes taught and practiced in a separate class. They may also be combined with speaking and pronunciation in an oral skills class or taught in a four-skills approach. I've chosen here to spend several chapters of this book pointing out the connections between and among skills, including some beyond the "big four."

Listening is interesting because it's both a skill and often the primary mode of second language input. Often, people learn to listen to and speak a language before acquiring literacy in it. Of course, to speak you need to understand, so listening can legitimately be considered the primary skill.

The problem with researching and teaching listening is that it goes on inside the learners' heads. We can never actually be sure that students understand everything—and often they don't need to. Perhaps we can never fully understand how learners get to their understanding, either. There are ways around these problems, however, and teachers and researchers have been teaching and probing listening for generations.

I have tried to balance classroom advice with the reasons for the advice, grounded in research evidence. I think it's important, if you want to grow as a teacher—and I presume you do if you are reading this book—that you have not only a bag of tricks, but a base from which to discuss your classroom with other teachers. I hope this book provides that base for listening instruction.

In the past, evidence of listening comprehension came from the answers that students gave to comprehension questions: *What do they need to buy? What time does the store open?* As we will see throughout this book, that approach has been largely replaced with **task-based listening**. The next chapter will both define *task-based listening* and consider what a listening program would look like. But first, a note about video.

A Word About Video

Throughout this book, not much distinction will be made between listening to aural input and watching video. The addition of a video component has been a major change in listening classes in terms of available content, but the basic principles of teaching listening hold. In general, many learners comprehend video texts better than aural-only ones (Nguyen & Newton, 2018). However, not all students will respond to multimedia lessons equally. Research seems to show that learners differ in their abilities to use visual information in a listening task (Sueyoshi & Hardison, 2005), or to use help options in listening software (Gruba, 2018). Moreover, adding a visual component also raises the issue of the need to teach about body language and gestures as clues to meaning.

Resources like blogs, wikis, and YouTube have exploded. For a very useful primer on these tools, see Duffy (2008).

Perhaps the most active aspect of video research is the research on captioning. Many researchers make a distinction between **captioning**—in which the text of the audio appears on the screen in the same language—and **subtitling**—in which the text is a translation (in another language) of the audio. Both captioning and subtitling have proven useful in word recognition, detail comprehension, and anxiety reduction. However, some research has found captioning to be more effective than subtitling (Hayati & Mohmedi, 2011). Furthermore, it is easy to understand how subtitling might be problematic in EFL classrooms in cases where the teacher cannot read the students' first language, or in multilingual classrooms.

Captioning is potentially useful in several ways. It connects sounds and/or writing with meaning. It also helps students to recognize words and possibly assists with vocabulary retention (Winke et al., 2013). However, Winke, Gass, and Sydorenko report that students' experiences with captions may differ based on native language and writing systems, content familiarity, and experience using captions in an educational context. Proficiency levels may also play a part, with beginners actually performing worse with captions, probably because of cognitive overload (Taylor, 2005). The usefulness of captioning may be especially diminished when the audio does not match the video, as is the case with many news stories.

The issue of cognitive overload has been partially addressed by **keyword captioning**, which presents important words or difficult vocabulary. Students have to read less. Results so far have been mixed, but it seems as if presenting difficult or low frequency words might be the best alternative if a keyword approach is used (Hsu et al., 2014).

1. Building a Task-Based Listening Program

A task-based listening program is made up of a series of listening tasks, so first we need to think about listening and then tasks. Following that, we will consider how to choose tasks and then consider student difficulties and feelings.

What Is Listening?

Contemporary listening approaches see listening as a kind of active model-building. Listening is not just a transfer of information from one person to another, a sort of aural/oral tennis match. Rather, listening is a process whereby the listener must interpret the speaker's intentions and reason for speaking, infer meaning, use context to make and form hypothesis as the conversation continues, and predict the direction the conversation will take. Thus, we can say that listening is a process of joint meaning-making.

Listening has usually been defined in classroom practice as comprehension. How well did the learners understand a piece of audio or the teacher's input? This often boils down to:

1. prepare (teach some words, find out what the students know about the topic)
2. listen for a few minutes
3. ask questions or go over the task
4. replay the audio
5. check again.

There is absolutely nothing wrong with this (with a few tweaks) as *practice*. Students need practice.

However, some (Richards, 2005, for example) think we can do better by going beyond "the comprehension approach." Richards argues for "the acquisition approach," in which students, after listening, work on the language in the listening text to improve their vocabulary, syntax, etc. Others (Vandergrift & Goh, 2012) focus more on metacognition (having students think about their learning) and strategies. Later chapters explore connections between listening and other skills and will look at pre- and post-task activities that go beyond comprehension.

As noted in the Introduction, listening instruction traditionally used questions to measure learner comprehension. These questions were often posed after the audio was played. This made the whole exercise a memory test. Students had to retain information that they didn't know they would be asked for. Some teachers understood the difficulty of this and began to give the questions *before* playing the audio. This is certainly an improvement and this method doubtless has its uses. However, in general, most listening instruction today is focused on tasks. The active aspect of tasks is probably the most noticeable in the classroom. Because the purpose of listening instruction is to learn to listen, teachers want to maximize that sort of practice. It is not a reading task or writing task, so the page or worksheet should require minimal reading (words, not long text) and minimal writing (check a box, circle the correct answer).

Listening Skills

In building a listening program, at some point the issue of which skills to teach must be decided. Taxonomies of skills are abundant. Lists of skills can go on for pages. To a large degree, you will be guided by the outcomes you must address. However, here is a very basic list of skills most students need:

- extracting specific terms and details in the input
- understanding explicitly stated information
- understanding implied information
- extracting a main idea
- matching what is heard to the possible answers, usually through the ability to paraphrase
- distinguishing main ideas from details
- understanding speaker attitudes and goals.

Some tasks to accomplish these goals will be offered later.

What Is a Task?

There has been a lot of research on tasks in general. (See Ellis, 2003, and Samuda & Bygate, 2008, for different perspectives.) I think it is fair to say that a consensus has developed that tasks are useful for language acquisition. Many curriculum developers (Long, 2015, for example) indeed put tasks at the center of the syllabus; students experience language learning through a series of clearly defined tasks.

While definitions of the word *task* vary, they all seem to share a few basic principles. The first is a focus on meaning rather than a focus on forms. A useful way to think about this is to put the students' lives at the center of the task. The learning is personalized and the students' lives and experiences are what is talked about. In terms of listening, this takes at least two forms. In some cases, the input that is listened to is a model for the speaking task that students will complete. Presumably the speaking task is relevant to the learners' lives, so although the listening task is not directly about the students, it does feed into a personalized speaking task. The other way listening tasks may be personalized is, of course, by asking students to answer, in speech or writing, direct questions related to the material: in a beginning-level time unit, for example: *What time did you get up this morning?* According to Van den Branden (2012), personalization is an important part of tasks because relevance leads to motivation.

The second aspect in any definition of the word *task* is usually preparation for a real-world task. That is, the pedagogical task mirrors a task the learners will encounter outside the classroom. To again use the example of a beginning-level unit on time, students hear times of train departures, write them all down, and choose which one is best for them (e.g., are they early risers or late risers?).

The third part of the definition of *task* is completion. There is a clear outcome for the task. Students know when they are done. A task outcome may be connected to a learning outcome. The idea of task completion may, then, be related to the assessment procedure for the unit.

Fourth, tasks are active. Learners do something, even if it's something they would only do in a classroom. They check a box, write a word, or follow a map. Ideally, tasks stimulate communication. This routinely happens after a listening task, when teachers and students discuss how students reached the answers they did. Programs may forget about the interactional aspect of listening, however. Listening is not just listening to a piece of audio or watching a video, but it also happens during speaking tasks when students share ideas.

A task, then, is relevant to the students' lives, relevant to their future needs, has a clear outcome or endpoint, and is active.

Choosing Tasks to Use

When we talk about real-world tasks, we need to talk about needs analysis. We need to figure out why and how learners will use the language and work backward from that knowledge in constructing classroom tasks. A matriculated college student will need to listen to lectures and also understand college staff in daily bureaucratic encounters. An immigrant needs to understand her supervisor.

But what does it mean to listen and understand? We need to go deeper. Needs analysis in listening takes into account the purpose for listening (social interaction, information gathering, entertainment, etc.). So, lecture listening and understanding instructions are both possible purposes. We can further break lecture listening into pieces, for example, by understanding transitions like *next* or signposts like *There are three important aspects....* Understanding when something is an aside and when it's central is also an important skill. Understanding instructions from a supervisor might entail getting a sequence correct or understanding which aspect of the immediate task is most important.

Needs analysis also takes account of the distinction between **transactional listening** (getting things done, as in making a purchase) and **interactional listening** (having a conversation with one's neighbor). Needs analysis further makes a distinction between **reciprocal listening** (the kind of listening we do conversationally) and **non-reciprocal listening** (the sort we do by ourselves, as when we listen to a podcast).

Once we have an idea of what students need, somebody (the teacher, the materials developer, the curriculum director) must decide on the input that students hear. There are some who insist that a task-based approach requires that the students be presented with authentic input, something taken from the real world. I don't accept this premise, partially because of the difficulty of using authentic materials at all proficiency levels and partially because I think there is value in pedagogical materials that scaffold a learner's development. (Also, the very concept of "authenticity" is a slippery one. See my critique of authenticity in Brown, 2011.) But if authenticity is paramount to you, by all means use authentic materials.

Things to think about in addition to authenticity when planning input are: (1) genre (for example, stories, conversations, podcasts); (2) familiarity with the topic and how motivating the topic is for your particular set of learners; and (3) amount and density of information (very important) given.

Another decision to make is whether you want learners to listen intensively or extensively. The short answer is probably "both." **Intensive listening** is that which focuses on a given piece of audio or text. This is the sort of listening done in textbooks and in most classrooms. The attempt is to understand as much as possible of what is heard and then to exploit the material for learning purposes. **Extensive listening** usually exists in a program in which students listen to longer passages such as a regular radio program or read along with graded readers. The purpose is to expose learners to as much language as possible. This is especially useful in EFL environments in which students are less likely to hear English in daily interactions. Two variations of extensive listening are narrow listening, in which students listen to a variety of material that is linked in subject matter, so that vocabulary is constantly recycled, and reading while listening, which combines reading a text with hearing it being read.

In principle, tasks should be graded in terms of difficulty. The classical model for grading oral and aural skills is that of Brown and Yule (1983), who proposed four factors to take into account when grading skills: speaker, listener, content, and support. **Speaker factors** include number of speakers (a monologue is, all things being equal, easier to keep track of than a dialogue), speed of speech (slower is usually easier), and familiarity of the speakers' accents (based on the dialect of English that is usually presented as the standard or model for the classroom). **Listener factors** include the role the listener plays (participant in a conversation or eavesdropper to others conversing), what the listener must do with the input (write a phrase, check a box), and the listener's interest and motivation. **Content factors** are grammar, vocabulary, discourse structure (which is related to genre), and background knowledge. **Support** includes visual aids or ancillary texts that help the learners understand what they are hearing.

Most of the decisions about which tasks to use will come from established goals of the program, future assessments, or perhaps from the textbook. In case you have to build a program, however, keep in mind the task definition and this very basic checklist for program planning:

- What will your student need to listen to in the future? Think about genres, topics. How familiar are students with the topics?
- What is motivating for your students? What's fun to listen to?
- How will the information received aurally be used? What will students do with what they hear?

- Who will the learners be interacting with, and in what roles? What roles are they hearing in the input?
- What are the students hearing? Is it conversational language, or a written text read aloud?
- Do your students need intensive or extensive listening, or both?
- How difficult cognitively are the tasks you are asking students to do?
- Are you mixing monologues and dialogues?
- How familiar is the speakers' model of English to the students?
- Do you want to, can you, control the speed of input?
- How are you providing support?

What Makes Listening Difficult?

There are a number of factors that affect the process of listening. Studies in the factors of listening have been done in two broad ways: first, through questionnaires and simulated recalls, which have looked back either at what students typically find difficult or found difficult in a particular listening task; and second, through factor-analytic studies that use statistics to look at the relative contributions of factors to listening scores.

If you ask students what they find difficult about listening, they will frequently cite the speaker's delivery speed or individual style (whether they hesitate a lot or have an accent). They will also say that vocabulary knowledge or simply not being able to divide the speech stream into recognizable words is a big issue. Goh (2000) found students had 10 problems with listening. Broadly speaking, these problems fell into three categories:

1. **Word recognition**—failing to pull individual words out of the speech stream, failing to recognize known words, getting caught up in trying to understand one word and losing the thread of the input
2. **Attention**—not being ready when the task started, having concentration problems
3. **Inability to form a coherent representation of what was heard**—seeing the trees, but not the forest.

Additional problems for learners, according to Chang and colleagues (2013), include grammar, long sentences (an aspect of attention), uninteresting topics (lack of motivation), anxiety, and absence of repetition or other task support.

Factor-analytic studies have given some insights into the individual differences that might facilitate or impede listening comprehension. Andringa and colleagues (2012) reported that the listening comprehension of learners of Dutch was strongly correlated with knowledge (of grammar and vocabulary, and an ability to break up the speech stream into individual words) and processing speed, but less strongly correlated with IQ, and only weakly correlated with memory. Vandergrift and Baker (2015) found that second language vocabulary knowledge had the strongest connection to listening ability in their study.

There are many ways to approach these findings, and a teacher's perspective will depend in part on her students' difficulties. I personally am struck by the centrality of vocabulary knowledge in these studies. If I were king, I would add a robust vocabulary component to listening classes. I will look more closely at the relationship between vocabulary and listening in Chapter 3.

Listening Anxiety

Because of these difficulties, many students find listening tasks terrifying (though this depends on linguistic and cultural groups—some students are more comfortable with listening/speaking than reading/writing). It seems terrifying to students because the words seem to fly by but students are trying to understand everything they hear, so they end up dropping farther and farther behind the speaker, and, eventually, they may give up. Lack of success breeds fear and anxiety. Elkhafaifi (2005a) argued for the existence of both generalized foreign language anxiety and specific listening anxiety, both of which have a negative effect on listening comprehension. Listening tasks may focus too much on correctness at the expense of learning to listen and learners may lack confidence, or worry about how they compare to their peers (Zhang, 2018). Foreign language anxiety continues to be researched, and classroom teachers know that it is a big problem.

So, what do we do? How can teachers alleviate anxiety in the classroom? Chang (2018a) recommends providing pre-listening support, allowing multiple listening, using a reading-while-listening approach, doing cooperative listening, and providing strategy instruction. These steps could all potentially work, but task-based listening also has much to offer in lowering anxiety. Task-based listening offers a series of steps that, if properly prepared and sequenced, can mediate difficulty and thus lower anxiety. Task-based listening also has the potential for individualization, which may also alleviate anxiety in that it allows learners to work at their own paces.

This chapter has taken up a number of issues involved in building a listening program, including some basic definitions, student needs, and difficulties. Next, we'll consider the listening lesson.

2. Building a Task-Based Listening Lesson

This chapter looks at the structure of a task-based listening lesson. A task-based approach implies a series of tasks that build on each other. This often manifests itself as a **pre-listening** stage, a **while-listening** (sometimes called during-listening) stage, including repetition of the input, and a **post-listening** stage. As previously stated, the response should reflect the nature of the task itself, so a listening task should require minimal reading and writing. An exception might be a dictation task, to which writing is fundamental.

Pre-Listening: Preparation, Purpose, Context

The purpose of the pre-listening stage of a lesson is to prepare learners to listen. Because time in any classroom is limited, teachers must take care to focus class energy on what is really needed. Typically, teachers do any of five things: (1) they activate schema—that is, raise learners' awareness of what they already know about the topic; (2) they provide some cultural background to the input; (3) they preview the questions; (4) they pre-teach vocabulary; and (5) they pre-teach grammar. They also provide a purpose and context for listening.

Schemata (plural of **schema**) are abstract mental representations based on our prior experience. In other words, after going to a restaurant and talking to servers hundreds of times, we construct in our heads a model for that encounter. We pretty much know what the server will say, and in what order. This is our background knowledge, in other words. Having a frame to put our conversations into lightens the mental load of interaction .Another way to think about schemata is through the notion of a *script*. We each have a script for familiar encounters that helps us understand how to react to those encounters. We assume the old and focus on the new and unusual (Long, 1989). In the classroom, teachers link what the students are going to hear to what they already know. Schema activation works because it reduces demands on a learner's attention. Employing what is already known makes processing easier.

Schemata are usually divided into content and formal schemata. **Content schemata** concern familiarity with topics and subject matter. **Formal schemata** concern knowledge of the language, and rhetorical and text structures (Nguyen & Newton, 2018). Because schema activation is deeply ingrained in our practice, appearing in any teacher's manual occupying a listening or four-skills textbook, I will only briefly note the research surrounding it. The main finding is that prior knowledge has a positive effect on comprehension. If a topic is familiar, or made familiar through an activity, a learner is more likely to be able to follow a listening passage. Culture is clearly an important aspect of topic familiarity. Several studies have shown that familiarity with history, religion, and popular culture, for example, affect listening comprehension (Brown, 2011).

Besides activating schemata, introducing the topic, and providing cultural background, teachers often direct the learners' attention to the questions they will have to answer to demonstrate comprehension.

The method of question preview has been shown to be effective. It has been compared to vocabulary preview by Berne (1995), Chung (2002) and Elkhafaifi (2005b). Berne (1995) reported a small advantage for a question preview over a vocabulary preview, although both helped comprehension, compared to no preview at all. Chung (2002) added a third possibility: a combined question-vocabulary preview. All three conditions—question preview, vocabulary preview, and a combined preview—were effective for low-achieving students, while the combined preview was markedly more effective for high achievers. The results also depended on the task. The combined preview was quite effective for open-ended questions, but the question preview and combined preview were equally effective for multiple choice questions. Elkhafaifi (2005b) found that both question preview and vocabulary preview were more effective than no preview at all, but that question preview was more effective on the first listening.

So, these work well to prepare students for listening:

- providing background knowledge of topic
- pre-teaching difficult features of the language to be heard (like vocabulary)
- previewing the questions to be answered.

In our daily lives, we usually have a purpose for listening and the task-based approach to listening tries to mirror this, giving learners a purpose for classroom listening. Pedagogically, this plays out in the standard division of listening tasks into:

- listening for the main idea or gist of the passage
- listening for specific information or details of the passage
- listening to infer the speaker's meaning or purpose for speaking.

An additional purpose for listening is quite common in our daily lives but sometimes ignored in the classroom: listening for pleasure, such as listening to songs or to videos. Giving students their purpose for listening beforehand allows them to focus on the information they need for that particular task and to ignore extraneous details. A useful classroom activity is to play the same piece of audio twice or three times, each with a different purpose. Thus, students learn to think about what they are listening for, rather than to try to understand everything. After all, in our native languages, we don't really understand one hundred percent of what we hear, and it is quite rare that we need to.

Again, in our daily lives, we usually not only have a purpose for listening, but a context. We have expectations about what we will hear based on the speaker, the place, the time, the topic, and what has gone before in the conversation (Brown & Yule, 1983). In terms of the classroom, giving students their purpose frequently is paired with providing a context. In commercial materials, this is often done in the instruction line: *Kim is talking to a friend about their weekend plans. Where are they going? Check the places.*

In the Classroom: Pre-Listening

Five things students should do before doing a listening activity in a textbook:

1. Look at the page. What's the topic?
2. Write five things you know about the topic.
3. Look at any word list that is provided. Check (or circle) the words you know.
4. Look at the pictures. Write words for what you see.
5. Look at the answer choices you have. What's the most important word in each choice?

While-Listening

Next in the series of tasks after pre-listening is the while-listening stage. Learners demonstrate comprehension by making minimal responses—checking, circling, writing one word or phrase. Reading, writing, and speaking are kept to a minimum.

Teachers differ in the number of times that they play the audio. General practice seems to be to give learners two or three times to listen, but this depends on proficiency level and difficulty of the input, of course. As noted above, it is a good idea to have the learners listen for different purposes, for example, for the main idea the first time and details the second. Research shows, perhaps not surprisingly, that repetition of the input increases comprehension scores. Chang and Read (2006) found that topic preparation in the L1 (in this case, Chinese for Taiwanese students) and repetition of the input were the most effective ways to prepare students for a listening task, with repetition working better for high-proficiency students. Iimura (2007) reported that repetition improved performance on both main idea and detail questions. Sakai (2009) also reported repetition facilitating comprehension. But how much repetition is optimal? King and East (2011) found that a single repetition was more effective than a slowed-down version of the input. However, Jensen and Vinther (2003) suggest that returns for repetition may diminish as soon as students hear it the second time, with fatigue setting in.

In the Classroom: While-Listening

If you are not using input from a textbook, here are some possible tasks. Main Idea Tasks:

- Decide what the topic is.
- Given a list of possible topics, decide which one is correct.
- Choose the correct summary statement from among several.
- Decide the function of the conversation: informing, inviting, or making recommendations?

Specific Information Tasks:

- List the topics talked about.
- Add extra information to the list of topics.
- Identify a series of steps or events.
- Fill in a grid or map.

Inference-Based Tasks:

- What's the context? How do you know?
- Who are the speakers and what is their relationship?
- Are there any emotions expressed? How do you know?
- Given a list, sort information that is true for each speaker.

Post-Listening

The post-listening stage might feature a metacognitive activity, in which students report how they got the answers they did (see Chapter 5). Very typical of a task-based approach to listening is the addition of a speaking activity linked to the topic of the input or acquisition activities that require learners to work with the language in the input.

In the Classroom: Post-Listening

Typically, the post-listening activity is a speaking activity tied to the theme or topic of the listening (see Chapter 7). Increasingly, teachers are working with transcripts of the lesson's audio to focus on the language the students have heard. Here's how to work with a transcript of the audio, usually provided in the Teacher's/Instructor's Manual of the textbook:

Working With Transcripts/Scripts of Listening Input:

- For pronunciation work: Learners mark stressed words and pauses. (See Chapters 3 and 4.)
- DIY Pair Work: One member of the pair (A) can delete words and hand the blacked-out script to a partner (B), who has to listen and write the missing words as A reads the script.
- Some learners find it useful to try to match the delivery of the audio as they read the script.
- If the passage has lots of examples of a particular grammatical structure, learners can search the transcript for them and then possibly put away the script to listen again, raising their hands when they hear the form.

3. Task-Based Listening and Vocabulary

This chapter considers issues that typically arise in the pre-listening stage of task-based listening, though, of course, individual teachers may choose to focus on different issues, as appropriate for their students. The main focus here will be on vocabulary, with a quick mention of grammar.

Vocabulary

I noted previously that vocabulary is a very important contributor to success in listening comprehension. There are three issues connected to vocabulary that are important to consider when thinking about task-based listening: recognizing known words, numbers of words necessary for successful listening, and learning new words through listening.

How Do Learners Recognize Words?

When we read English, words are separated by white spaces on the page. The listener has no such advantage. The speech stream rushes in, and it is the listener's task to break it up into words, phrases, and sentences. As the words are held in working memory, they are enriched with our prior knowledge of the world, the situational context, and the co-text (what has been said already, plus predictions of what might be said). Knowledge of the language system, including grammar and the rules of discourse, also plays a part (Anderson & Lynch, 1988). This general process is known as **decoding**.

The process of finding the breaks between the words is called **lexical segmentation**. Learners use their knowledge of the language, along with clues like stress and beginning sounds, to activate their vocabulary knowledge.

A moment's reflection will remind us that this process is not simple. Sounds have effects on neighboring sounds. Sounds get pushed together, deleted, and otherwise manipulated for ease of articulation. This is not so much "sloppy speech" as following the sound system of the language being spoken. Redistribution or resyllabification is a common process. For example, when the typical speaker of English pronounces *blue ink*, they insert a /w/

sound between the ending vowel of the first word and beginning vowel of the next: *blue wink*. A competent speaker/listener of English basically ignores the insertion and hears *blue ink*. A learner of English may mishear. For example, my niece's younger son regularly heard that I lived *in Ohio*. He assigned the /n/ to the second word and asked me when I was going back to Nohio. (He has since grown up and I have moved to California, so this is no longer an issue.) Some problems learners might encounter along these lines are:

- **Assimilation**: One word has an effect on the other sound (*ten men* sounds like *temmen*)
- **Deletion**: A sound gets dropped (*every* sounds like *evry*)
- **Insertion**: A sound gets added (*athlete* becomes *athalete*)
- **Weak vowels**: Vowels in stressed syllables are clearly pronounced, while vowels in unstressed syllables sound like a neutral sound made in the middle of the mouth (a schwa), or unstressed vowels may disappear completely.

Here's where authentic language is useful. Learners might read a transcript of authentic audio and circle where they hear these processes at work.

Another problem is that learners often rely on their first language. They may substitute sounds in their first language for sounds in their second language, activating incorrect guesses that may be reluctant to change, even with repeated listening (Cross, 2009; Field, 2008). **Phonotactics** is the concern with the probabilities involved in sounds appearing at different places in a given language. For example, in English we can end a word with the consonant cluster *nt*, but we cannot begin a word with the same cluster. Having this information, which we acquire implicitly for our native language, is obviously very useful for breaking up the speech stream. It helps us know where one word ends and the other begins. This is one example of language similarity working in some learners' favor. If someone is trying to learn English, and their language has similar phonotactic rules, they start ahead of learners whose language does not share those rules. However, there is some evidence that students can be taught this information if their language has different rules. English and Arabic differ in their phonotactic rules. For example, while you can't start an English word with *bw* or *dl*, you may in certain dialects of Arabic. Al-Jasser (2008) taught Saudi-Arabian undergraduates English phonotactics to help them segment English speech. The group that received the training improved in reaction time and error rate over the group that did not. That is, they recognized words quicker and made fewer mistakes recognizing words.

Even if learners correctly segment the input, there remains the problem of assigning meaning to the word. Word activation is affected by how frequent the word is, how close the word is to other words that sound or mean the same, and what words have been raised in the learner's mind by what has already been heard. First language and individual vocabulary knowledge play key roles in word activation. Learners may substitute a known word for an unknown one, potentially derailing comprehension.

Teachers frequently encourage students to listen for "key words." Students may, consequently, listen for nouns, their idea of a key word. They may need to be encouraged to listen for verbs as well (Graham & Santos, 2013).

If learners are successful in segmenting the input and activating their knowledge to assign a correct meaning to the word, they must then put words together with other words into phrases and sentences to comprehend what they have heard. All this happens, of course, in an amazingly short time, as the input continues unabated. What do learners do when they have trouble making sense of the input? As many teachers will recognize, learners will frequently use their prior knowledge. Often, just one stressed word in the input is enough to activate schemata (Wu, 1998). This is more often than not a failed strategy that sends learners off-track. It is more useful for learners to learn a wider variety of strategies (see Chapter 5), or to learn more words.

In the Classroom: Pre-Teaching Vocabulary

Three things teachers should think about when pre-teaching vocabulary:

1. Make sure the words you teach are important to the task at hand.
2. Worry about the context in which students will hear the words. Don't try to teach all the meanings of a word. Teach only the meaning that is relevant to the task.
3. Make sure students recognize the pronunciation of the words.

In the Classroom: Vocabulary Activation Activities

Siegel (2018) provides some ways to activate schema for a listening task. These are some ways to focus on words or phrases in the input:

- Brainstorm words related to the topic and ask students to check off the words they actually hear.

- Focus on the context of a conversation. Given participants and setting, what do students expect to hear?
- Focus on the genre or function: What is the situation? A telephone call? A lecture?
- Anticipate what will happen next based on playing a portion of the audio.

In the Classroom: Lexical Segmentation

A number of sources provide classroom activities that practice breaking up the speech stream.

Goh and Wallace (2018) suggest three activities: counting words, identifying intonation units, and marking stressed syllables.

Counting words gives students practice in recognizing how connected speech operates. The teacher plays a dialogue or other piece of connected speech or reads a passage. After raising schema for the topic, the teacher plays or reads one sentence at a time. Students count the number of words. The input is repeated to allow students to check and revise. Then a transcript of the input is handed out, and there is a self-check stage. The teacher may then read the transcript as the students follow along; the teacher may point out the examples of connected speech.

An **intonation unit** is a thought group (think of meaningful phrases, like *the big red dog* and *jumped the fence*) separated from other thought groups by pauses. The point of this exercise is to recognize speech as organized into these intonation units, rather than as individual words. First, the students listen to the full text. Then the transcript of the text is handed out and students mark the places where they hear a pause. Then they check with an answer sheet and, finally, read along with the answer sheet. After marking the boundaries, more advanced students can also mark, with arrows, the rise and fall of intonation that they hear. The rise and fall of the intonation will happen at the boundaries between the intonation groups and will help mark the most important words in the text. The students may also mark the stressed syllables in the text.

Field (2008) presents a useful set of exercises for making students aware of the phonological processes of English. Here are some things that he encourages teachers to practice with their students:

- Identify strong and weak syllables, making students aware that the strong/weak pattern is very common in English.

- Recognize where one syllable becomes part of the next word (*went in* sounds like *when tin*).
- Identify function words that get reduced in speech (articles, modal verbs, conjunctions, auxiliary verbs like *be, have, do*).
- Identify reduced forms (*whaddaya* for *what do you*)

The next chapter considers how pronunciation and listening fit together.

Dictation and dictogloss are also useful activities for recognizing words in input. They will be addressed in Chapter 6 with task-based listening and literacy.

Vocabulary Size and Listening

Folse (2004) has been a consistent advocate for the central role of vocabulary in language acquisition, and Vandergrift (2006) argued for the importance of vocabulary in listening development, specifically. Staehr (2009) reported that vocabulary size accounted for 49 percent of the listening comprehension scores in his study. The better the vocabulary knowledge his subjects displayed, the better their comprehension scores. Mecartty (2000) compared the roles of vocabulary knowledge and grammatical knowledge for his subjects and concluded that, while both were important to comprehension, only lexical knowledge contributed to both reading and listening comprehension in a statistically significant way.

How do you count words? One way is to use the idea of a **word family**, which includes the root word (*work*) and its grammatical inflections and derivational forms: *works, worked, rework*, etc. Word families are arrayed by researchers into "bands" of the 1,000 most common words, the 2,000 most common words, and so on. Frequency is measured using computer-generated corpora that are built by inputting language of interest—spoken language, written language, or a mix of both (e.g., the Contemporary Corpus of American English, COCA).

How many words do we need to know? Researchers generally agree that a learner has to know 95–98 percent of the words to understand a text. They use the word **coverage** to tie word families to those percentages. So, X number of words provides Y% of coverage of the material. Nation (2006) investigated the number of word families needed to understand unplanned spoken English. His corpus was made up of talk radio transcripts and conversations among friends and family. He found that 3,000 word families, plus some proper nouns, would cover 95 percent of the language in his corpus, and

6,000–7,000 would provide 98 percent coverage. Since 95 percent coverage would still mean seven unknown words per minute, he recommended 6,000 to 7,000 words as a base for understanding conversations. Adolphs and Schmitt (2003) concur that 6,000–7,000 word families would allow for 98 percent coverage. Van Zeeland and Schmitt (2013) found that listeners could understand passages with 90 percent coverage, but got higher scores at 95 percent coverage and higher scores yet at 98 percent coverage. They then concluded that 95 percent (2,000–3,000 word families) might be a good target for comprehension of informal spoken narratives and that 98 percent coverage might be appropriate in cases where a high degree of comprehension is desired, or if difficult material is presented.

While speech is characterized by the use of relatively simple vocabulary and, face to face, by the use of extra-linguistic cues like gestures, students still need a fair number of words. Vocabulary acquisition is a long process and learners must encounter a given word multiple times and actually engage with the word, including learning how it sounds. Just teaching a word once before a listening task probably won't do much good in the long run, which is why I have presented pre-teaching vocabulary as one of many pre-listening task possibilities earlier. Pre-teaching vocabulary *can* help immediate comprehension (Alavi & Janbaz, 2014; Jafari & Hashim, 2012), but student language development would benefit most from a focus on vocabulary acquisition within the larger listening program.

Learning Vocabulary Through Listening

Some researchers have wondered whether listening can provide input for growth in vocabulary knowledge and in grammatical knowledge, so this section will look at the issue of incidental learning of vocabulary while listening. **Incidental learning** refers to the process of learning something that was not intended to be learned; the knowledge is "picked up."

While it seems that we do pick up vocabulary effortlessly in our first language, in a second language, it is much more difficult. The first problem is, as previously discussed, that we need to understand 90–98 percent of the words in the input to even begin to guess at meaning. While reading, that is perhaps not so much an issue: the words stay fixed on the page. While listening, the words fly by, often in a form we do not recognize from the vocabulary list. The second problem is that we may not encounter that word again, or may hear it again three weeks later. Here, listening may have some advantage over reading, in that we tend to use common words and set phrases in speech. It is possible that we could pick up some common idioms through listening. However, although they disagree on exact numbers, most researchers say that we need to encounter a word from six to more than twenty times to learn it (Cervatiuc, 2018). Laufer and Hulstijn (2001) go farther, arguing that learners actually have to become involved with a word in the specific ways of *need, search*, and *evaluation* to acquire it. The learner has to have a *need* to retain the word, a *need* to *search* for it or look it up, and a *need* to see how well the meaning has been understood through some sort of *evaluation* task.

As can be imagined, all these issues set a high bar for incidental vocabulary acquisition through listening. Brown and colleagues (2008) compared gains in vocabulary knowledge through reading, reading while listening, and listening. All three conditions led to some gains, but the listening-only condition was the least effective. Vidal (2011) compared incidental acquisition using reading and listening tasks and came to the same result: while both conditions led to gains in knowledge, gains from listening were lower than gains from reading.

The conclusion is that students can learn vocabulary incidentally from listening, but it is not a very effective way to increase knowledge.

In the Classroom: Vocabulary Resources

This is not the place to discuss extensively the many tools available to teachers for teaching vocabulary. A very useful site is the "Vocabulary Resources" section of Norbert Schmitt's website (https://www.norbertschmitt.co.uk/vocabulary-resources), which has links to just about all you'll need, including a link to the Compleat Lexical Tutor site (https://www.lextutor.ca), which is the essential foundation for further research in this area.

Grammar and Task-Based Listening

This section considers whether listening can improve grammatical knowledge. Here, the issue is not incidental learning, but rather implicit learning versus explicit learning. **Implicit learning** occurs when someone has a feel or sense for something; they may not be able to verbalize their knowledge. This largely describes the knowledge we have of our native language before we start explicitly learning its grammatical rules in school. **Explicit learning** is intentional or hypothesis-driven. It involves awareness and we can verbalize what we have learned.

DeJong (2005) created a complex study to test if learners who listened for meaning could acquire the grammatical rules of an artificial language. He found that learners who completed only the listening tasks were indeed able to learn the target grammar and able also to induce some rules from the input without having been explicitly taught those rules.

The problem with learning grammar implicitly from listening is that it is inefficient. It is quite possible for learners to comprehend what they hear without processing the grammatical structures in it. Often, students can pull out key words, make inferences, and get the message.

Explicit teaching of grammar sometimes occurs in the context of dictation or dictogloss tasks (these tasks will be discussed in Chapter 6). Another example of explicit teaching of grammar is the task-based approach of Willis and Willis (2007). They begin with having the learners listen to audio of fluent speakers doing the task that they will do. A transcript of the recording is then provided and students work on a grammatical or vocabulary feature in the text.

In most classes, grammar probably is most often addressed in either the pre-listening stage or in post-listening tasks involving the use of transcripts.

In the Classroom: Pre-Teaching Grammar

Here are some things to consider when teaching grammar as part of a listening lesson:

1. Teach the structures that are needed to understand the input. Ask yourself if any structures need to be taught at all.
2. Consider teaching structures as lexical bundles, useful phrases. Teach the phrases *Turn right/left*, not the grammatical label of imperative.
3. Write the topic on the board. Ask students to brainstorm sentences they expect to hear.
4. During a second or third listening, focus on structures by asking students to raise their hands when they hear examples.
5. To review, ask students to construct dialogues from one-sentence examples of the structure.

The next chapter builds on some of the issues in vocabulary to talk about pronunciation work in the listening lesson.

4. Task-Based Listening and Pronunciation Instruction

In this chapter, we consider the relationship between task-based listening and pronunciation instruction. Teachers may elect to work with concepts of phonetics and phonology to alert students to the processes that may interfere with lexical segmentation, or pulling words out of the speech stream. They may use some of the same concepts to work on students' receptive skills before working on productive pronunciation skills.

Listening and Pronunciation

Let me first clarify what we are talking about in this chapter: the relationship between listening and pronunciation is largely a receptive one. (The production of sounds will not be addressed here.) Here's a model Marc Helgesen and I worked on years ago. The examples are not exhaustive. This chapter focuses on the upper left side of the box, on **receptive accuracy**. (The right side of the box will be discussed in Chapter 7.)

Receptive Accuracy	Productive Accuracy
Discriminate sounds in speech	Focus on forms in speech and
Intensive reading: skim, scan	writing: pronunciation and grammar
Intensive listening: main idea, details	(including work with transcripts)
Use of morphology, syntax to	Edited writing
understand message	Careful speech, public speaking
Receptive Fluency	**Productive Fluency**
Extensive reading	Conversation
Extensive listening	Communicative activities
Narrow listening	Diaries, journals

It has been a common-sense notion for years that one has to hear a distinction before that distinction can be reliably produced. There is little hard evidence of a causal relationship between the two, but in probably the most important work in the field of teaching pronunciation, Celce-Murcia and colleagues (2010, p. 391) come down on the side of a link between perception and production and say that the ability to discriminate "distinctions" in a language is "critical." Paulston and Bruder (1976, p. 82) say that "pronunciation practice cannot in any real sense be divorced from listening practice."

Teachers have some options within the context of the listening lesson to present and practice information about pronunciation. For example, there can be pre-teaching of information about syllable and stress, as shown in Chapter 3. The presentation and practice can come between repetition of the listening, as a way to draw attention to forms in the input. Teachers may also elect to do pronunciation work in the post-listening stage, as preparation for a speaking activity. Here, they are thinking about students' production.

Though the research base is small, some have empirically investigated the relationship between listening and pronunciation. Trofimovich (2011) re-analyzes data from two studies. One is a study done in Canada with Francophone learners of English in Grades 3 and 4 (Trofimovich et al., 2009). The experimental group participated in a comprehension-based program. Learners in this program only read or listened to English. They worked independently, at their own pace, reading material supported by audio. They did not participate in lessons or take tests, speak to other students in English, or receive teacher feedback. The control group participated in a standard aural-oral language program with tasks, activities, and some supporting reading/writing practice.

The students were tested at the ends of Grades 3 and 4. Tests of their pronunciation showed that, on this measure, the two groups were equal. Just listening and reading were sufficient for pronunciation learning.

Analyzing results from the Trofimovich and colleagues (2007) study, Trofimovich (2011) reports that large amounts of listening were correlated with greater accuracy in producing the *th* sound in *mother*.

Cakir (2012) and Motallebi and Pourgharib (2013) offer some support for the connection between pronunciation and listening. Both studies used a combination of extensive reading and listening to improve learners' pronunciation. However, in each case, the variables were confounded, insufficiently separated, to my mind, so that listening was not clearly the only reason that the students improved. In both cases, there seemed to be explicit teaching of phonetics, which might have been equally effective or more effective than listening for improving pronunciation.

In the Classroom: Pronunciation in the Listening Classroom

Activities that develop the links between listening and pronunciation include:

• Working on pauses, thought groups, stress, and intonation. In addition, things that are not there—unstressed sounds and reduced forms—are important.

• Working with thought groups through transcriptions of the audio available in the teacher's manual. Either dialogues or reading passages from the textbook can be used. Beginning students can mark the pauses the teacher makes as she reads the transcription and they follow along. More advanced students can predict where the pauses are and confirm their predictions as the teacher reads. A good speaking activity is to put the students in pairs to practice the passage. To make things interesting, the students can change some content words. They first listen for the changed words and then read the new passage. Another possible change to this procedure is that the teacher can give a hint about the number of pauses. Teachers can also construct worksheets with alternative sentences (two choices are probably enough). Which did you hear, A or B?

> A: *My sister, who is an optician, lives in California.* OR
> B: *My sister who is an optician lives in California.*

> The answer here depends on pausing at the commas. In the first one, I have one sister. In the second, I have more than one. I'm differentiating the one who is an optician from the other(s).

• Working with stress using transcripts. Students circle or underline stressed words. Beginners might simply follow along with a transcript showing stressed words and then practice reading the passage in pairs. Alternatively, a gapped version of a short passage might be handed out. The gaps correspond to the stressed words. Students write the words and then work with a partner to check. In addition, teachers can work with intonation by having students draw lines to indicate whether the voice goes up or down.

• Making students aware of how function words like prepositions, articles, pronouns, and auxiliary verbs are unstressed. The pairs and groups *him/them, or/are, a/of/have, in/an/am/and* are all frequently confused. This is a difficult issue that won't resolve itself immediately, but it is useful to bring awareness of unstressed words and practice discriminating among them. Teachers may provide a gapped handout with choices so that students predict answers based on their grammatical knowledge and then listen to check/confirm. Here is an example:

Is the woman ____ the red dress Sally or Jennifer?

(a) on   (b) in   (c) an

- Working with reduced phrases such as *whaddaya (what do you)* and *wanna (want to)*. This is a good idea for listening but may not be for production. Here, the teacher can dictate the reduced form, and the students write the full form. Gapped listening can also be done with worksheets. Again, teacher reads the reduced form and students write the full form. Alternatively, the full and reduced forms can be presented side by side and students can practice with choral and pair reading.
- Jones (2018) reminds us to include physical gestures to pronunciation work. When working on stress, adding a physical element like pulling on rubber bands, opening and closing fists, and standing and sitting all make the learners feel the stressed and reduced syllables.

Other pronunciation practice possibilities are:

- Count the number of sounds in a word.
- Odd one out: which sound is different among the three?
- Same or different?
- Assign sounds a number. Is it 1 or 2?

Next, we will investigate strategies and metacognitive instruction. In doing so, we will look at how learners can help themselves during their listening tasks.

5. Task-Based Listening: Strategies and Metacognition

We move in this chapter to something used in all stages of the lesson: strategies and metacognition. **Strategies** are techniques or actions used to facilitate learning. In other words, strategies are ways to improve or organize one's learning. O'Malley and Chamot (1990) made the classic division of language learning strategies into these categories: cognitive, metacognitive, and socio-affective. **Cognitive strategies** range from simple note-taking to inferring something based on background knowledge. **Metacognitive strategies** are those that encourage earners to think about their thinking and about the task at hand. When learners make a plan for listening and then evaluate how well that plan is working (Are they understanding the audio?), they are using metacognitive strategies. **Socio-affective strategies** speak to the anxiety and emotions inherent in listening. How are the learners going to approach what they often see as a difficult task? **Metacognition** is thinking about thinking. It is an influential way to look at how learners approach listening.

We expand on all of these statements in this chapter. Following a look at strategies and metacognition, we will look at one specific use of strategies, in academic listening.

Strategies

Vandergrift and Cross (2018a) point out that it is difficult to separate metacognitive strategies and cognitive strategies. The former provide a framework in which the latter are deployed. One important cognitive strategy used in the pre-listening stage is elaboration, in which students expand what they already know from personal experience, knowledge of the world, knowledge of the topic, and other schemata to prepare to understand the listening text. Possible cognitive strategies in the while-listening stage include use of cognates to link first language knowledge to the second language, use of logical inferencing, and application of background knowledge to the developing understanding of the text.

Metacognitive strategies are those that organize learning. They include planning, monitoring, and evaluating what is heard (Cross & Vandergrift,

2018). Teachers in the pre-listening stage might, for example, ask the students to make a plan in which they predict, based on the topic, what they expect to hear. As they listen, they ask themselves if their predictions have been useful and make any necessary changes to the plan based on a revised understanding of the content. As a class, there might be a more formal evaluation stage in which students share their experiences.

Socio-affective strategies typically are most often used in interactive listening with another speaker. They help manage feelings, address motivation, and lower anxiety (Vandergrift & Cross, 2018b). The more social strategies include asking for clarification where something is not understood, back channeling (giving feedback to the speaker that you are listening, as in *uh huh*). There will be more on interactive strategies in Chapter 7. **Affective strategies** can be used in the typical listening class as well. These strategies speak directly to the common fear that individual students often exhibit to listening. Their use tends to be highly individualized. Some students do not need them at all, while others benefit from classroom discussions of how to lower anxiety and increase motivation.

Metacognition

In many classrooms, strategy training is done in the context of a metacognitive approach to listening. At its most basic, **metacognition** is thinking about thinking, and a metacognitive approach urges learners to consider how they listen and how they may improve. Processes associated with metacognition include planning, monitoring, and evaluations (Goh, 2018a).

Metacognitive knowledge includes **person knowledge** (factors the students experience while listening, problems encountered, beliefs about listening, self-efficacy); **task knowledge** (knowledge of the nature of listening, external factors involved in listening, skills needed); and **strategy knowledge** (the strategies available for listening and how to choose the best ones for the task at hand (Goh, 2018a).

In the context of a listening lesson, a metacognitive approach offers opportunities for learners to develop a listening plan based on knowledge of the topic and other considerations brought up during the pre-listening stage. It provides opportunities for awareness-raising activities and strategy use during the lesson. In the while-listening stage, at the end of each repetition of the input, the teacher allows students to discuss how their plans are working and how they might better comprehend the material. Learners might check off strategies that they are using on a list of possible strategies or answer prompts about their listening process. They might keep listening journals or diaries (Vandergrift & Goh, 2012).

Rather than replacing the strategy approach to listening, the metacognitive approach builds on it, encouraging the use of strategies at appropriate times of the lesson, as well as putting strategies in the context of building knowledge of how to listen.

Some Evidence

Strategies and their use have been extensively studied and, generally, their use has been shown to be helpful in listening comprehension, although some results have depended on age and proficiency of the students (Brown, 2011). What seems clear is that if a teacher wants students to use strategies, those strategies must be taught overtly (Graham et al., 2011). It also seems clear that a program that presents strategies in a principled fashion is probably the most useful way to accomplish the goal.

For example, Graham and Macaro (2008) taught a number of interconnected strategies to adolescent learners: predicting, confirming predictions, identifying key words in the input, recognizing familiar words, inferring from prior knowledge, and breaking up the speech stream into recognizable words. They presented the strategies as interconnected, not as a series of independent strategies. Students receiving this organized strategy training scored higher on tests of comprehension compared to students who did not receive the training—and did so even six months later.

Vandergrift and Tafaghodtari (2010) also took a coordinated approach to teaching strategies in their study of university students. While the approach led to benefits for the group at large, the less proficient students benefited the most from strategy training. The approach involved predicting and checking predictions, individual and peer reflections on performance, and whole-class discussions of strategy use. Partly because the subjects of the study were university students with some language learning experience, instruction in strategies was less explicit than in the previous study.

In the Classroom: Strategy and Metacognitive Instruction

While, overall, strategy use and a metacognitive approach to listening have shown themselves to be useful tools for improving comprehension, much depends on the ages and proficiency of students, as well as their prior experience of language learning. Since a coordinated approach to strategy instruction is a time-consuming business, requiring some knowledge and commitment from the teacher, it is probably a good idea to do a needs analysis and pre-test of your students' knowledge and use of strategies before beginning a program. One useful tool is the Metacognitive Awareness Listening Questionnaire (MALQ) (Vandergrift & Goh, 2012, pp. 286–287), which measures how aware students are of aspects of the listening process. There are also numerous strategy-use checklists available online through which students can self-report their knowledge and use of strategies.

Even if you find that your students are fairly sophisticated in their strategy use, it is probably a good idea to reinforce a metacognitive approach to listening through activities and class discussions.

Academic Listening: Learning From Lectures

Academic listening has traditionally been virtually synonymous with lecture listening. This, of course, is a great simplification. University students need to be able to discuss the readings with their peers, and they need to talk to university staff about late-adding classes, changing meal plans, and returning books to the bookstore. (See Lynch, 2011, for an expanded conceptualization of academic listening.)

Nevertheless, lecture listening is very important and remains the focus of most commercial materials and overviews of the topic (Goh, 2018b). Most lecture-listening classes and materials present a number of strategies for comprehension and note-taking, divided into the categories of understanding colloquial, unplanned speech of professors and understanding the typical structure of lectures.

A fair amount of research has been conducted on lecture comprehension. Background knowledge, vocabulary, the attention necessary to listen for as long as two hours, and speech rate all contribute to making lectures difficult. Perhaps the most challenging aspect of lecture comprehension is forming an overall mental representation of the lecturer's purpose and how that purpose will be fulfilled. This representation involves understanding the form the lecture will take (comparison/contrast, chronological, problem/solution), and then dividing that form into recognizable main ideas and supporting details. For that reason, researchers have frequently focused on **discourse markers**. These have been divided into macro-markers (*Today I'm going to...*, *There are three ideas to consider ...*) and micro-markers (*OK, Next, Now*). Jung's studies (2003; 2006) showed the importance of discourse markers generally. The markers helped form both cause-effect and sequential relationships between ideas. Students who heard a lecture with markers retained more information than students who heard the same lecture with the markers stripped out.

Based on the research, textbooks have largely focused on teaching the macro-markers, but some attention has been paid to the micro-markers.

As Lynch (2011) points out, more attention is beginning to be paid to "two-way" academic listening and to lecturers' use of multimedia, among other topics. However, it would seem that in the classroom, the equation of academic listening and lecture listening remains.

In the Classroom: Academic Listening

Here are some basic strategies to practice in a listening class (Rost & Wilson, 2013). I have taken their list (the words in bold type) and tied it to the stages of the listening lesson and offered some classroom possibilities.

Pre-listening

Planning: Learners need to develop a plan for listening. They need to understand what it will take to successfully complete the task. What are the goals of the task? What are the steps involved? In real life, we use the context of the listening situation to help us understand what to listen for.

Planning can be a constant in the pre-listening stage: draw attention to purpose and context for the listening. Teachers should get into the practice of developing plans and evaluating them after the first listening and at the end of the lesson.

While listening

Focusing attention: Learners need to be able to concentrate on the input and on the task. They must learn to push away distractions and to focus selectively on input aspects such as key words. Their plan helps with this focus, but students must also be flexible, which is why monitoring (checking understanding) is important.

Though this is a strategy typically used while listening, pre-listening work helps. Engage students in brainstorming what words they expect to hear based on the task, the look of the page, etc. Between repetitions of the audio, solicit from students what words they heard.

Monitoring: Learners have to constantly update their plan. How well are they understanding? Do they need to revise their initial understanding? Emotions play a role here: students cannot let anxiety get the better of them when there are problems presented by the input.

Again, between listening opportunities, perhaps in pairs, give students an opportunity to figure out what they need to listen for the next time.

Evaluating: Monitoring leads to evaluation. As the answers are checked, or a repetition of the input is allowed, learners check themselves and identify problems they had.

It's important to always include a feedback session after the listening.

Inferencing: Learners use inferencing to guess at meanings of new words and to predict what they will hear next, based on context. Inference fills in the learners' blanks in linguistic, cultural, and speaker knowledge.

Teachers need to be sure to provide practice in inferencing and prediction.

Elaborating: Elaborating also fills in blanks. Learners use their prior knowledge to connect what they are hearing with what they know about the world.

A reminder: pre-listening helps here by activating schema.

Post-listening

Collaborating: Learners in an interactive situation, such as a conversation or speaking task, work with each other to seek clarification and confirmation. They use backchannel behaviors (e.g., *uh huh*) to show engagement.

This strategy is most often used in interactive listening (see Chapter 7). Teachers should allow students to work collaboratively during listening because it's not cheating; it's practice.

Reviewing: Learners may use summary, repetition, note-taking, and translation to help store the knowledge gained during the listening task.

Interestingly, a listening class sometimes doesn't have much homework, but maybe it should.

6. Task-Based Listening, Reading, and Writing

Reading and writing tasks are typically done in the while-listening stage. This chapter addresses three topics: extensive listening/listening while reading, dictation, and dictogloss.

Extensive Listening and Listening While Reading

Extensive listening is a broad term that signifies a focus on listening to long, connected discourse for meaning. Typical input comes from the internet (TED talks are especially popular), TV, radio, video, and audiobooks (including graded readers). The listening happens inside or outside of class. One kind of extensive listening is listening while reading or reading while listening; this is probably the most researched aspect of extensive listening. Listening while reading (LWR) means exactly what it says: students listen to audio of a book as they read.

Chang's (2009) study of Taiwanese university students compared LWR and listening only. The students read two stories. While the listeners scored 10 percent higher on two tests, compared to the reader/listeners, learners liked the LWR activity much better. They thought it was easier and thought it was shorter and more interesting. They also felt that they paid better attention.

Woodall (2010) compared two groups that read a children's novel where one group read the book, while the other read while listening to a professional recording of the book. The LWR group outscored the reading-only group in half of the quizzes given.

Chang and Millet (2014) found that LWR led to improvement in listening fluency. Both listening-only and LWR groups performed significantly better on tests of listening comprehension, compared to those reading only.

Chang (2018b) surveyed other studies, arguing that extensive listening improves reading speed and comprehension as well as listening attitude (including lowering anxiety). She recommended reading or listening to at least one book a week for the full benefits of extensive listening to be felt. (It's a little unclear, but I assume that she means one graded reader.)

Chang also recommended a follow-up activity such as listening again without the book or, in the case of a video, listening without the transcript, followed by listening with the transcript and then without it.

Many teachers organize extensive listening and specifically LWR as an independent activity, with each student choosing to listen to something they find personally motivating. Others have the entire class read/listen to the same material. In this case, pre-listening activities can be done to help comprehension.

Extensive listening in general is potentially a very useful part of a listening program, especially if learners can choose their own materials. I think that care has to be taken to be balanced, however. It seems to me that some, not all, extensive listening advocates make an equivalence between learning the first and the second language. We've heard this idea for 40 years, despite compelling evidence that first and second language acquisition are different in important ways. There has been fairly substantial agreement for some time that at least some attention needs to be paid for language to be acquired (Norris & Ortega, 2000): you can't just let input wash over you and expect to learn a language. This is why Reinders and Cho (2010) added a noticing aspect to their study.

Extensive listening, all kinds, is great practice, and there might be some incidental learning that takes place (vocabulary, for example). Extensive listening is motivating, and that's great, but it is no accident that most studies of extensive listening come from situations where learners are adult false beginners (students who have studied English for six years or more). Looking at the wider picture, I'm skeptical of programs in which extensive listening is the only source of input. I'm not saying that beginners cannot benefit from extensive listening. Given proper materials, they can. Nor am I saying that students do not need to listen to longer stretches of discourse. They do; they need more than the ten minutes of audio in the textbook. So, try extensive listening if you haven't already. But make it just one tool in the box.

In the Classroom: Setting Up an Extensive Listening Program

The Extensive Listening section of Rob Waring's website (http://(http://www.robwaring.org) is the best place to start reading about extensive listening. There are really two issues involved—the classroom infrastructure and, because extensive listening is by definition individualized, student choice of materials.

By "classroom infrastructure," I mean resources. Is your program going to be based on graded readers, on reading while listening, or on websites such as ELLO (English Listening Lab Online), Voice of America, BBC World Service, or Spotlight Radio? These websites are all pitched to learners so they are not authentic. That's good. You don't want learners trying to understand fast idiomatic English at first. You want them to be able to understand about 95 percent of the words. If the learners can understand 95 percent of the input, TED talks have proven to be very popular sources for listening classes.

Regarding choice of materials, on his site, Waring has a document called Starting Extensive Listening that is written at a level appropriate to intermediate-level students. (It is written to Japanese learners because that's where Waring works.) Waring gives the following advice to students starting out with extensive listening:

- They should be able to understand 90 percent of the content.
- They should be able to understand over 95 percent of the vocabulary and grammar.
- They should be able to listen and understand without stopping the audio.
- They should enjoy the content!

Getting a program set up will take some time. Students will need to look through materials to find their comfort zone, answering the issues listed. You will need to decide how to assess their work. How will you give a grade? Will you reward the amount they listen to? (I would vote for that.) Is there some other criterion that you find more worthy of reward? My feeling is that a united front among teachers is a good thing. It's probably useful to talk to your colleagues to develop goals and standards.

Dictation

Dictation is a technique that has been evaluated differently at different times. In some eras, it has been an important means to learning, but in others, it has been discounted as mechanical and mindless (Stansfield, 1985). Recently, dictation has made something of a comeback, in light of a general desire to work with language more closely in the listening lesson. As Nation (1991) points out, dictation is an accuracy-oriented technique that helps learners focus on phrases and clauses. While Nation (1991, p. 12) says that dictation is most effective "when it involves known vocabulary that is presented in unfamiliar collocations and constructions," we have seen that dictation is often also useful for pronunciation work (see Chapter 4). Given the poor sound-to-symbol correspondence in English (a.k.a. weird spelling), it is also useful for practicing the forms of words.

The efficacy of dictation has been tested in several studies. In an Iranian study, Kiany and Shiramiry (2002) compared two groups, one whose input was from a textbook and another whose input was the textbook plus 11 dictations over the length of the course. The dictations were based on the textbook's reading passages and conversations. Students who did the dictations scored better on a standardized listening test, perhaps unsurprisingly, since they got more listening practice.

Rahimi (2008) compared the effect of dictation among groups of Iranian university students. The group that completed dictations improved in grammar, vocabulary, reading, and listening comprehension, while the control group showed improvement only in vocabulary. Rahimi attributes this to both groups being translation majors whose overall program stressed vocabulary acquisition. The study is interesting because Rahimi actually went over the corrected dictations in class, which elevated the dictation from a testing activity to a teaching activity. Dictation is often criticized as mere testing, but this study shows it can be more. Rahimi admits that results can be criticized because the dictation group actually had more class time (about 10 minutes per session) than the control group. There was also no immediate post-test; rather, that post-test was delayed for 10 months, meaning that subjects could have improved through other means, like attendance at language institutes.

Reinders (2009) compared dictation to two grammar-oriented tasks whose purpose was to reconstruct a whole text from memory. One group took notes on the text and reconstructed it individually, and the other reconstructed the text collaboratively from notes. The dictation group heard the text in smaller chunks (80–100 words) and had to type it. The measurement was correct use of the grammatical structure called "negative adverbs with subject/verb inversion," as in *Never have I seen anything like that*. The dictation group and the collaborative group both improved their knowledge of the structure compared to the individual group.

Kuo (2010) used partial dictation of a radio program in Taiwan to improve her university students' listening comprehension. The radio program was transcribed and words deleted. Students listened and filled in the blanks.

It was a partial dictation because Kuo utilized beginning and ending letters to give clues to the students.

Kazazoglu (2013) reported on a study of Turkish high school students. One group heard teacher-read dictations and another heard tape-recorded dictations of the same material. Kazazoglu found that the tape-recorded dictation led to many more (for one text almost twice as many) word errors than the teacher-led dictations, which is attributed to the unfamiliarity of the native speaker voice on the audio. Students also made fewer errors on the longer of the two passages, which suggests than more context leads to better listening comprehension.

There is clearly more to know about the efficacy of dictations in the classroom, but studies such as these point in some interesting directions for future research.

In the Classroom: Dictation

The procedure for using dictations is:

1. Teacher reads sentences or text.
2. Students write.
3. Teacher reads twice more, with students checking their production after each repetition.
4. Teacher presents handout or other visual with the correct answers.
5. Teacher collects papers to see what needs work or lets students keep dictations in their portfolios.

Alternative: For mixed-ability groups, teacher provides a gapped/closed version of the passage to beginners, while more advanced students are challenged to produce the passage from scratch.

Here are some ideas for communicative dictations (Brown, 2011):

1. Find the differences between the spoken text and what is on the handout. This can be done as a whole-class activity or in pairs, where the listener corrects the "mistakes" of the speaker.
2. Jigsaw listening: partners get two versions of the same text and reconcile them. Alternatively, this is a narrative activity in which the pairs combine their information to make a story.

3. Students write the dictated sentences, but add their own content (personal information) at cued points.
4. The teacher holds up a picture and says a mixture of true and false statements about it. Students write the correct sentences and correct the false ones.
5. The teacher reads sentences and students decide whether they are true or false, writing their guesses in columns under *I think...* and *I don't think....* (Trivia is a good topic here.)

Dictogloss

Probably most "dictation" today is in the form of **dictogloss**, or what is often called **dicto-comp**. While in traditional dictation, the goal of the task is to perfectly replicate the input, in dictogloss the focus is less on perfect replication than on meaning.

In dictogloss, students listen to a passage read at normal speed, take notes, and use those notes to work with a partner to reconstruct the passage as best they can. Their reconstruction does not have to be perfect, just true.

The underlying rationale for dictogloss is that, in order to acquire language, learners need to notice the gap between what they know and the target form. Thus, dictogloss can be a way to teach grammar, but it is also an efficient technique for improving listening comprehension (El-Esery, 2016; Prince, 2013). Dictogloss combines listening, writing, and discussion, with a goal to students noticing gaps in their knowledge that they and their teachers can work on. The very act of reconstructing the text leads to some fairly sophisticated discussion of language—*Should we write X or Y?*

Vasiljevich (2010) reports on the use of dictogloss not to raise awareness of grammar, but specifically as a means to improve listening comprehension. Vasiljevich recommends adding a substantial warm-up period before the text is presented, including pre-teaching vocabulary and introducing the topic through preview questions that activate learners' schemata. Vasiljevich also inserts a discussion period between the second and third listening so that students can see what they need to focus on to complete the task. Finally, rather than present the full text for students to check, Vasiljevich suggests a "reconstruction checklist" with points awarded for important vocabulary and ideas (fully included, partially included, or not included at all). Pairs swap reconstructions and use the checklist as peer assessment.

In the Classroom: Dictogloss

This is the procedure for dictogloss:

1. The teacher reads the text twice at normal speed. For the first listening, students just listen.
2. Students write the words or phrases they can.
3. In pairs, students pool their answers and reconstruct the text to the best of their knowledge. It won't be perfect.
4. The class discusses and compares answers.

Alternative: Student-to-student dictogloss
Alternative: Use pre-listening questions to help students activate schema about the topic.
Note: You will really need to stress that their answers should focus on meaning, not on exact replication. This needs constant reinforcement.

7. Task-Based Listening and Speaking

Speaking tasks are typically done in the post-listening stage, though they are also common in pre-listening and while-listening (e.g., when answers for the first listening are checked before the input is repeated). This chapter will consider the nature of interactive listening, the nature of a good speaking task and interactive listening skills. This chapter will focus on the right side of this box.

Receptive Accuracy	Productive Accuracy
Discriminate sounds in speech Intensive reading: skim, scan Intensive listening: main idea, details Use of morphology, syntax to understand message	Focus on forms in speech and writing: pronunciation and grammar (including work with transcripts) Edited writing Careful speech, public speaking
Receptive Fluency	Productive Fluency
Extensive reading Extensive listening Narrow listening	Conversation Communicative activities Diaries, journals

Interactive Listening

Most of our daily listening is probably interactional or two-way listening. Of course, that depends on our living situation and amount of contact with others, but generally we go through life speaking to and responding to others. The speaker typically has a goal or goals to accomplish. That may be to obtain information, to form or care for social bonds, or any other of a variety of goals. The listener must select relevant information, attend to the information, and interpret the speaker's message. The listener provides oral or non-verbal feedback to the speaker: checking and signaling comprehension, seeking clarification, and negotiating meaning. Thus, as previously noted, listening is a highly active process through which people jointly construct meaning. There are also sometimes "overhearers" involved in the setting of a two-person conversation (another friend, the rest of the students in a class in which one student is asking the teacher a question, for example).

The negotiation of meaning between and among learners has been a staple of the communicative approach to language teaching for 40 years. Whether you believe that the best way to acquire languages is through lots of comprehensible input, through the interaction itself, or through actively examining student output, interactive listening provides a flexible means toward those ends.

As Goh (2018c) points out, however, the listening aspect of interactive listening needs to be made explicit. She says that the discussion skills and strategies that listeners and speakers may use will need to be taught or reviewed. Students will need model phrases for feedback, and they will likely need to be pre-taught vocabulary.

The Good Speaking Task

The communicative approach to language learning ushered in a strong emphasis on interaction in the classroom that has lasted 40 years. Instead of everyone listening to the teacher, students talk to each other in pairs or groups. We sometimes forget that these speaking tasks are also listening tasks. As will be shown, listeners make use of a large number of strategies to understand speakers. First, however, I want to quickly look at what researchers have seen as good listening tasks.

Pica and colleagues (1993) looked at the literature on speaking tasks that foster interaction, comprehension, feedback, and interlanguage modification (language growth, in other words). These are all things we want out of a speaking task. They found that tasks with these goals are characterized by certain factors:

1. A jigsaw structure: each participant has some information that the other doesn't have and they must convey that information for the task to be successfully completed.
2. Participants must have the same goals.
3. There must be only one possible outcome to the task.

Keck and colleagues (2006) performed a meta-analysis of 14 studies and found that tasks in which students interacted with each other led to gains in language learning. Confirming Pica and colleagues' (1993) findings, jigsaw and information gap tasks were seen to be particularly effective. Task essentialness was another factor that led to effective leading. **Task essentialness** means that learners must use the structure or words that the teacher wants them to use (as opposed to saying *Yes* or *No* or nodding their head). It is difficult to construct tasks that force the learner's hand in this way, but, to the extent that one can, the students benefit.

To the list of effective task elements, we should also add pre-task planning and repetition of tasks (Ellis, 2005). Pre-task planning—giving students enough time to think about how they will perform the task—has been shown to increase fluency (students speak with fewer hesitations) and complexity of language (measured by use of difficult grammatical structures). The results are mixed for accuracy, partially because as students use more complex language, they tend to make more mistakes. Task repetition is simply doing the task again, with a different partner. We can also use task cycles, in which the same language is used in each step.

In the Classroom: Interactive Listening and Post-Listening Tasks

What are common goals for post-listening activities? We have advocated using transcripts to work on vocabulary, sounds, and grammar, focusing on accuracy. Many times, we want students to focus on fluency, to orally practice the language they have heard, focusing on the functions and speech acts, like asking for information, giving directions, etc. We might want students to look critically at something in the input, forming an opinion.

Thinking on a global level, you might want to consider the functions that Vandergrift and Goh (2012) provide for post-listening activities. Which is your purpose for the activity, or is there another?

- **Meaning elaboration**: By this they mean knowledge transfer from the students' understanding of listening input to speaking or writing tasks. This may include synthesis, analysis, and evaluation of what they have heard.
- **language analysis**: This is similar to Richard's "listening for acquisition." Learners pay attention to grammar, vocabulary, pronunciation, etc., in the text/transcript.
- **Planning and editing**: Learners use metacognition to reflect on their experience and performance.

Drilling down to a practical level, here are some things to consider when planning speaking tasks:

1. **Two-way tasks**, such as jigsaw or information-gap tasks where each participant has something to contribute, generate more language than

one-way tasks like telling a story. That being said, mix one-way and two-way tasks for variety.

2. **Closed tasks**, for which there is only one outcome, tend to feature more complex language and language "recycling" as learners try to reach an acceptable conclusion.

3. If students have the same goal for the activity, the task tends to be more effective. Goals might need to be negotiated during the planning stage.

4. Allow for pre-task planning. Just a few minutes can affect the successful completion of the task.

5. Consider repeating the task with a different partner.

6. Consider cognitive demands. Is the task appropriate for your learners' stage(s) of development?

7. For many of the reasons stated, *Talk about* ... and *Discuss...* are not tasks.

8. Students need support. If they don't know how to say something, they probably won't say it. On the board, include key phrases or sentence stems that learners can use to complete the task. Yes, you've "taught" them, but there's a lot going on in communication. They need some friendly reminders. This includes support in negotiating meaning, to which we turn next.

In the Classroom: Providing Support for Interactive Listening Activities

Interactive listening relies on the use of a number of strategies on the part of the listener. The listener must find ways to check understanding, confirm hypotheses, and indicate lack of understanding. Here, from Brown (2011), is a synthesis of what are called "reception strategies" from the work of Rost and Ross (1991), Vandergrift (1997), and Farrell and Mallard (2006), along with some possible ways to accomplish the strategy:

- Ask for repetition of a word, phrase, fragment, or chunk (*Could you repeat that? I'm sorry, I didn't catch that. Again please?*)
- Ask for a paraphrase of a segment of speech (*I didn't understand the part about X. Could you explain X?*)
- Ask for the meaning of an individual word or phrase (*What does X mean? I don't know the meaning of X.*)
- Ask about "the first part," etc. (*I didn't understand the first part. I didn't understand the part that came after X.*)
- Use non-verbal continuation signals (nodding the head)

- Use non-verbal signs signaling lack of understanding (frowning, questioning look on face)
- Use verbal continuation signals, backchanneling (*Uh huh, Yeah, Mm*)
- Use hypothesis testing: specific questions about the text to confirm understanding, rephrasing of the text to confirm (*Did you mean X? So...*)
- Use forward inference: specific questions about established facts (*He left? So they were alone?*)
- Repeat parts of the text, either to indicate understanding, or, with questioning intonation, lack of understanding (*I see, an expensive car. A car?*)
- Indicate lack of global understanding: (*Huh? I'm lost!*)
- Fake it: continuing to listen, waiting to see if understanding emerges (nodding, using backchanneling)

Teachers can provide a classroom poster with simple, common strategies such as these and, circulating during pair or group work, can refer struggling learners to the poster. Here are the expressions we have taught for many years in the *English Firsthand* series (Helgesen et al., 2010, back flap):

- How do you say ___ in English?
- Could you repeat that?
- Excuse me?
- Pardon?
- How do you spell (that)?
- What does ___ mean?
- I don't understand yet.
- Did you say ___ or ___?

In the Classroom: Some Basic Speaking Activities

Remember three things:

1. Students must know how to say what they want to say. Provide stem sentences, key phrases, and feedback language on the board. Your textbook probably has a box of example sentences for the chapter. Project it.
2. Provide a goal. *Discuss* is not a goal.
3. Provide motivation. Turning tasks into games is one way to do this.

Here are some basic activities that fit a variety of situations:

- Finding connections: Students make connections between pictures, words, each other, etc. The main task is to link two or more things. This could be telling a story that incorporates the pictures or includes the words. It could involve finding commonalities between the students.
- Things that are the same: Students find three to five similarities or differences between people, cities, etc.
- Things that are different: Students find differences in two pictures or cartoons.
- ABC game: Groups think of an item beginning with each letter of the alphabet, repeating the previous ones. Last person points to the next participant to keep people on their toes. No writing.
- Ordering: Students put pictures in order to form a story. Order strip stories, individual sentences, or paragraphs that form a story.
- Find someone who...: The teacher writes on the board, dictates, or gives out a list of about 10–12 items. (e.g., *Find someone who has a cat.*) Students must find a member of the class that can answer *Yes* to each item on the list. Once a person answers *Yes*, that person cannot be used again. However, as many questions as necessary can be asked to get a *yes*.
- Combining: Students work with another group and share the results of the task. They decide which is the better solution. Or combine results.
- Chalkboard race: Teams line up and, individually, in turn, write examples of categories that the teacher calls out, in a given time.
- Fluency workshop (Maurice, 1983): The entire class lines up in two lines, face to face. They are given a topic. One member of the pair talks to their first partner on that topic for 90 seconds (or for an appropriate time). The other member talks for the same amount of time. Then, one line shifts to the right, so that everyone has a new partner. The time is reduced (from 90 seconds to 60, for example). Each partner has a chance to repeat their story, polishing it. The lines move once more to the right and the time is further reduced (to 30 seconds, for example).

There are many teacher reference books with useful ideas for speaking activities and I encourage you to make yourself familiar with some.

Conclusion

Here we are at the end. I'm pretty confident that what I've told you gives you a good base.

It's what, after 40 years of teaching, I think you need to know, at least. I hope you've gotten a lot of classroom ideas and that you understand, through some research, a little better why we do what we do.

When I give presentations, I always try to link what I say directly to the classroom. Inevitably, someone will come up and ask, essentially, "What about my classroom?" I (gently, I hope) point out that I teach in my classroom and not in theirs. Some people find that a disappointing answer. Sorry, I haven't found a better one in 40 years. An individual classroom is an incredibly complicated place and you incontestably know yours best. Take what's here and think about it. Apply the things you can directly. If others are a little off for you, fix them, or break them and start over. The point of this book is to give you a tool. Now, get out there and use it!

REFERENCES

Adolphs, S., & Schmitt, N. (2003). Lexical coverage and spoken discourse. *Applied Linguistics, 24,* 425–438.

Alavi, S. M., & Janbaz, F. (2014). Comparing two pre-listening supports with Iranian EFL learners: Opportunity or obstacle. *RELC Journal, 45,* 253–267.

Al-jasser, F. (2008). The effect of teaching English phonotactics on the lexical segmentation of English as a foreign language. *System, 36,* 94–106.

Anderson, A., & Lynch, T. (1988). *Listening.* Oxford, UK: Oxford University Press.

Andringa, S., Olsthoorn, N., van Beuningen, C., Schoonen, R., & Hulstijn, J. (2012). Determinants of success in native and non-native listening comprehension: An individual differences approach. *Language Learning, 62* (Suppl. 2), 49–78.

Berne, J.E. (1995). How does varying pre-listening activities affect second language listening comprehension? *Hispania, 78,* 316–329.

Brown, G., & Yule, G. (1983). *Teaching the spoken language.* Cambridge, UK: Cambridge University Press.

Brown, R., Waring, R., & Donkaewbua, S. (2008). Incidental vocabulary acquisition from reading, reading-while-listening, and listening to stories. *Reading in a Foreign Language, 20,* 136–163.

Brown, S. (2011). *Listening myths: Applying second language research to classroom teaching.* Ann Arbor: University of Michigan Press.

Cakir, I. (2012). Promoting correct pronunciation through supported audio material for EFL learners. *Energy Education Science and Technology Part B: Social and Educational Studies, 4*(3), 1801–1812.

Celce-Murcia, M., Brinton, D., & Goodwin, J. (2010). *Teaching pronunciation: A course book and reference guide (2nd ed.).* New York: Cambridge University Press.

Cervatiuc, A. (2018). Incidental learning of vocabulary. In J. L. Liontas (Ed.), *The TESOL encyclopedia of English language teaching.* New York: John Wiley & Sons. DOI: 10.1002/9781118784235.eelt0819.

Chang, A. C.-S. (2009). Gains to L2 listeners from reading while listening vs. listening only in comprehending short stories. *System, 37*, 652–663.

Chang, A. C.-S. (2018a). Affect in second language listening. In J. L. Liontas (Ed.), *The TESOL encyclopedia of English language teaching*. New York: John Wiley & Sons. DOI: 10.1002/9781118784235.eelt0580.

Chang, A. C.-S. (2018b). Extensive listening. In J. L. Liontas (Ed.), *The TESOL encyclopedia of English language teaching*. New York: John Wiley & Sons. DOI: 10.1002/9781118784235.eelt0564.

Chang, A. C.-S., & Millet, S. (2014). The effect of extensive listening on developing L2 listening fluency: Some hard evidence. *ELT Journal, 68*, 31–40.

Chang, A. C.-S., & Read, J. (2006). The effects of listening support on the listening performance of EFL learners. *TESOL Quarterly, 40*, 375–394.

Chang, A. C.-S., Wu, B. W.-P., & Pang, J. C.-L. (2013). Second language listening difficulties perceived by low-level learners. *Perceptual and Motor Skills, 116*, 415–434.

Chung, J.-M. (2002). The effect of two advance organizers with video text on the teaching of listening in English. *Foreign Language Annals, 35*, 231–241.

Cross, J. (2009). Diagnosing the process, text, and intrusion problems responsible for L2 listeners' decoding errors. *The Asian EFL Journal Quarterly, 11*(2), 31–53.

Cross, J., & Vandergrift. L. (2018). Metacognitive listening strategies. In J. L. Liontas (Ed.), *The TESOL encyclopedia of English language teaching*. New York: John Wiley & Sons. DOI: 10.1002/9781118784235.eelt0589.

DeJong, N. (2005). Can second language grammar be learned through listening? *Studies in Second Language Acquisition, 27*, 205–304.

Duffy, P. (2008). Engaging the YouTube Google-eyed generation: Strategies for using Web 2.0 in teaching and learning. *Electronic Journal of eLearning, 6*(2), 119–131. Retrieved from http://www.ejel.org/issue/download.html?idArticle=64

El-Esery, A. M. (2016). Dictogloss-based activities for developing EFL learners' listening comprehension. *International Journal of English Language Teaching, 4*(10), 42–51.

Elkhafaifi, H. (2005a). Listening comprehension and anxiety in the Arabic language classroom. *Modern Language Journal, 89*, 206–220.

Elkhafaifi, H. (2005b). The effect of prelistening activities on listening comprehension in Arabic learners. *Foreign Language Annals, 38*, 505–513.

Ellis, R. (2003). *Task-based language learning and teaching*. Oxford, UK: Oxford University Press.

Ellis, R. (Ed.) (2005). *Planning and task performance in a second language.* Amsterdam: John Benjamins.

Farrell, T. S. C., & Mallard, C. (2006). The use of reception strategies by learners of French as a foreign language. *Modern Language Journal, 90,* 338–352.

Field, J. (2008). *Listening in the language classroom.* Cambridge, UK: Cambridge University Press.

Folse, K. (2004). *Vocabulary Myths: Applying second language research to classroom teaching.* Ann Arbor: University of Michigan Press.

Goh, C. (2000). A cognitive perspective on language learners' listening comprehension problems. *System, 28,* 55–75.

Goh, C. C. M. (2018a). Metacognition in second language listening. In J. L. Liontas (Ed.), *The TESOL encyclopedia of English language teaching.* New York: John Wiley & Sons. DOI: 10.1002/9781118784235.eelt0572.

Goh, C. C. M. (2018b). Academic listening. In J. L. Liontas (Ed.), *The TESOL encyclopedia of English language teaching.* New York: John Wiley & Sons. DOI: 10.1002/9781118784235.eelt0595.

Goh, C. C. M. (2018c). Listening activities. In J. L. Liontas (Ed.), *The TESOL encyclopedia of English language teaching.* New York: John Wiley & Sons. DOI: 10.1002/9781118784235.eelt0604.

Goh, C. M., & Wallace, M. (2018). Lexical segmentation in listening. In J. L. Liontas (Ed.), *The TESOL encyclopedia of English language teaching.* New York: John Wiley & Sons. DOI: 10.1002/9781118784235.eelt0603.

Graham, S., & Macaro, E. (2008). Strategy instruction in listening for lower-intermediate learners of French. *Language Learning, 58,* 747–783.

Graham, S., & Santos, D. (2013). Selective listening in L2 learners of French. *Language Awareness, 22,* 56–75.

Graham, S., Santos, D., & Vanderplank, R. (2011). Exploring the relationship between listening development and strategy use. *Language Teaching Research, 15,* 435–456.

Gruba, P. (2018). Technology for teaching listening. In J. L. Liontas (Ed.), *The TESOL encyclopedia of English language teaching.* New York: John Wiley & Sons. DOI: 10.1002/9781118784235.eelt0442.

Hayati, A. M., & Mohmedi, F. (2011). The effect of films with and without subtitles on listening comprehension of EFL learners. *British Journal of Educational Technology, 42,* 181–192.

Helgesen, M., Brown, S., & Wiltshier, J. (2010). *English Firsthand 1.* Hong Kong: Pearson Asia.

Hsu, C.-K., Hwang, G.-J., & Chang, C.-K. (2014). An automatic caption filtering and partial hiding approach to improving the English listening comprehension of EFL students. *Educational Technology & Society, 17,* 270–283.

Iimura, H. (2007). The listening process: Effects of type and repetition. *Language Education and Technology, 44,* 75–85.

Jafari, K., & Hashim, F. (2012). The effects of using advance organizers on improving EFL learners' listening comprehension: A mixed method study. *System, 40*(2), 270–281. DOI: 10.1016/j.system.2012.04.009.

Jensen, E. D., & Vinther, T. (2003). Exact repetition as input enhancement in second language acquisition. *Language Learning, 53,* 373–428.

Jones, T. (2018). Materials development for teaching pronunciation. In J. L. Liontas (Ed.), *The TESOL encyclopedia of English language teaching.* New York: John Wiley & Sons. DOI: 10.1002/9781118784235.eelt0697.

Jung, E. H. (2003). The role of discourse signaling cues in second language listening comprehension. *Modern Language Journal, 87,* 562–577.

Jung, E. H. (2006). Misunderstanding of academic monologues by nonnative speakers of English. *Journal of Pragmatics, 38,* 1928–1942.

Kazazoglu, S. (2013). Dictation as a language teaching tool. *Procedia–Social and Behavioral Sciences, 70,* 1338–1346.

Keck, C. M., Iberri-Shea, G., Tracy-Ventura, N., & Wa-Mbaleka, S. (2006). Investigating the empirical link between task-based interaction and acquisition: A meta-analysis. In J. M. Norris & L. Ortega. (Eds.), *Synthesizing research on language learning and teaching* (pp. 91–131). Amsterdam: John Benjamins.

Kiany, G. R., & Shiramiry, E. (2002). The effect of frequent dictation on the listening comprehension ability of elementary EFL learners. *TESL Canada Journal, 20,* 57–63.

King, C., & East, M. (2011). Learners' interaction with listening tasks: Is either input repetition or slower rate of delivery of benefit? *New Zealand Studies in Applied Linguistics, 17,* 70–85.

Kuo, Y. (2010). Using partial dictation of an English teaching radio program to enhance EFL learners' listening comprehension. *Asian EFL Journal, 47,* http://asian-efl-journal.com/PTA/October-2010-Kuo.pdf.

Laufer, B., & Hulstijn, J. (2001). Incidental vocabulary in a second language: The construct of task-induced involvement. *Applied Linguistics, 22,* 1–26.

Long, D. R. (1989). Second language listening comprehension: A schema-theoretic perspective. *Modern Language Journal, 73,* 32–40.

Long, M. (2015). *Second language acquisition and task-based language teaching.* Malden, MA: Wiley.

Lynch, T. (2011). Academic listening in the 21st century: Reviewing a decade of research. *Journal of English for Academic Purposes, 10*, 79–88.

Maurice, K. (1983). The fluency workshop. *TESOL Newsletter, 17*, 429.

Mecartty, F. H. (2000). Lexical and grammatical knowledge in reading and listening comprehension by foreign language learners of Spanish. *Applied Language Learning, 11*(2), 323–348.

Motallebi, S., & Pourgharib, B. (2013). The impact of audio stories (listening skills) on pronunciation of EFL learners. *Journal of Language Sciences & Linguistics, 1*, 1–6.

Nation, I. S. P. (2006). How large a vocabulary is needed for reading and listening? *The Canadian Modern Language Review, 63*, 59–82.

Nation, P. (1991). Dictation, dicto-comp, and related techniques. *English Teaching Forum, 29*(4), 12–14.

Nguyen, C.-D., & Newton, J. (2018). Schemata in listening comprehension. In J. L. Liontas (Ed.), *The TESOL encyclopedia of English language teaching.* New York: John Wiley & Sons. DOI: 10.1002/9781118784235. eelto592.

Norris, J. M., & Ortega. L. (2000). Effectiveness of L2 instruction: A research synthesis and quantitative meat-analysis. *Language Learning, 50*, 417–528.

O'Malley, J. M., & Chamot, A. U. (1990). *Learning strategies in second language acquisition.* Cambridge, UK: Cambridge University Press.

Paulston, C. B., & Bruder, M. N. (1976). *Teaching English as a second language: Techniques and procedures.* Boston, MA: Little, Brown.

Pica, T., Young, R., & Falodun, J. (1993). Choosing and using communicative tasks for second language instruction and research. In G. Crookes & S. M. Gass. (Eds.), *Tasks and language learning: Integrating theory and practice* (pp. 9–34). Clevedon, UK: Multilingual Matters.

Prince, P. (2013). Listening, remembering, writing: Exploring the dictogloss task. *Language Teaching Research, 17*, 486–500.

Rahimi, M. (2008). Using dictation to improve language proficiency. *The Asian EFL Journal, 10*(1), 33–47.

Reinders, H. (2009). Learner uptake and acquisition in three grammar-oriented production activities. *Language Teaching Research, 13*, 201–222.

Reinders, H. & Cho, M. (2010). Extensive listening practice and input enhancement using mobile phones: Encouraging out-of-class learning with mobile phones. *TESL-EJ, 14*(2). https://tesl-ej.org/wordpress/issues/volume14/ej54/ej54m2/.

Richards, J. C. (2005). Second thoughts on teaching listening. *RELC Journal, 36*, 85–92.

Rost, M., & Ross, S. (1991). Learner use of strategies in interaction: Typology and teachability. *Language Learning, 41*, 235–268.

Rost, M., & Wilson, J. J. (2013). *Active Listening*. Harlow, UK: Pearson Education.

Sakai, H. (2009). Effect of repetition of exposure and proficiency level in L2 listening test. *TESOL Quarterly, 43*, 360–372.

Salehzadeh, J. (2006). *Academic listening strategies: A guide to understanding lectures*. Ann Arbor: University of Michigan Press.

Samuda, V., & Bygate, M. (2008). *Tasks in second language learning*. Basingstoke, UK: Palgrave Macmillan.

Siegel, J. (2018). Teaching bottom-up and top-down strategies. In J. L. Liontas (Ed.), *The TESOL encyclopedia of English language teaching*. New York: John Wiley & Sons. DOI: 10.1002/9781118784235.eelto597.

Staehr, L. S. (2009). Vocabulary knowledge and advanced listening comprehension in English as a foreign language. *Studies in Second Language Acquisition, 31*, 577–607.

Stansfield, C. W. (1985). A history of dictation in foreign language teaching and testing. *Modern Language Journal, 69*, 121–128.

Sueyoshi, A., & Hardison, D. (2005). The role of gestures and facial cues in second language listening comprehension. *Language Learning, 55*, 661–699.

Taylor, G. (2005). Perceived processing strategies of students watching captioned video. *Foreign Language Annals, 38*, 422–427.

Trofimovich, P. (2011). Language experience in L2 phonological learning: Effects of psycholinguistic and sociolinguistic variables. *International Review of Applied Linguistics, 49*, 135–156.

Trofimovich, P., Gatbonton, .E. & Segalowitz, N. (2007). A dynamic look at L2 phonological learning: Seeking psycholinguistic explanations for implicational phenomena. *Studies in Second Language Acquisition, 29*, 407–448.

Trofimovich, P., Lightbown, P. M., Halter, R., & Song, H. (2009). Comprehension-based practice: The development of L2 pronunciation in a listening and reading program. *Studies in Second Langauge Acquisition, 31*, 609–639.

Van den Branden, K. (2012). Task-based language education. In A. Burns and J. C. Richards (Eds.), *The Cambridge guide to pedagogy and practice in second language teaching* (pp. 132–139). Cambridge, UK: Cambridge University Press.

Vandergrift, L. (1997). The Cinderella of communication strategies: Reception strategies in interactive listening. *Modern Language Journal, 81*, 494–505.

Vandergrift, L. (2006). Second language listening: Listening ability or language proficiency? *Modern Language Journal, 90*, 6–18.

Vandergrift, L., & Baker, S. (2015). Learner variables in second language listening comprehension: An exploratory path analysis. *Language Learning*, *65*, 390–416.

Vandergrift. L., & Cross, J. (2018a). Cognitive listening strategies. In J. L. Liontas (Ed.) *The TESOL encyclopedia of English language teaching*. New York: John Wiley & Sons. DOI: 10.1002/9781118784235.eelto582.

Vandergrift, L., & Cross, J. (2018b). Socio-affective listening strategies. In J. L. Liontas (Ed.), *The TESOL encyclopedia of English language teaching*. New York: John Wiley & Sons. DOI: 10.1002/9781118784235.eelto594.

Vandergrift, L., and Goh, C. C. M. (2012). *Teaching and learning second language listening: Metacognition in action*. New York: Routledge.

Vandergrift, L., & Tafaghodtari, M. H. (2010). Teaching L2 learners how to listen does make a difference: An empirical study. *Language Learning, 60*, 470–497.

van Zeeland, H., & Schmitt, N. (2013). Lexical coverage of L1 and L2 listening comprehension: The same or different from reading comprehension? *Applied Linguistics, 34*, 457–479.

Vasiljevich. Z. (2010). Dictogloss as an interactive method of teaching listening comprehension. *English Language Teaching, 3*, 41–52.

Vidal, K. (2011). A comparison of the effects of reading and listening on incidental vocabulary acquisition. *Language Learning, 61*, 219–258.

Willis, D., & Willis, J. (2007). *Doing task-based teaching*. Oxford, UK: Oxford University Press.

Winke, P., Gass, S., & Sydorenko, T. (2013). Factors influencing the use of captions by foreign language learners: An eye-tracking study. *Modern Language Journal, 97*, 254–275.

Woodall, B. (2010). Simultaneous listening and reading in ESL: Helping second language learners read (and enjoy reading) more efficiently. *TESOL Journal, 1*(2), 186–205.

Wu, Y. (1998). What do tests of listening comprehension test? A retrospection study of EFL test-takers performing a multiple-choice task. *Language Testing, 15*, 21–44.

Zhang, X. (2018). Listener anxiety. In J. L. Liontas (Ed.), *The TESOL encyclopedia of English language teaching*. New York: John Wiley & Sons. DOI: 10.1002/9781118784235.eelto587.

Printed and bound by CPI Group (UK) Ltd, Croydon, CR0 4YY

13/04/2025

14656506-0002